BEI GRIN MACHT SICH IHR WISSEN BEZAHLT

- Wir veröffentlichen Ihre Hausarbeit, Bachelor- und Masterarbeit

- Ihr eigenes eBook und Buch - weltweit in allen wichtigen Shops

- Verdienen Sie an jedem Verkauf

Jetzt bei www.GRIN.com hochladen und kostenlos publizieren

Bibliografische Information der Deutschen Nationalbibliothek:

Die Deutsche Bibliothek verzeichnet diese Publikation in der Deutschen National-bibliografie; detaillierte bibliografische Daten sind im Internet über http://dnb.d-nb.de/ abrufbar.

Dieses Werk sowie alle darin enthaltenen einzelnen Beiträge und Abbildungen sind urheberrechtlich geschützt. Jede Verwertung, die nicht ausdrücklich vom Urheberrechtsschutz zugelassen ist, bedarf der vorherigen Zustimmung des Verlages. Das gilt insbesondere für Vervielfältigungen, Bearbeitungen, Übersetzungen, Mikroverfilmungen, Auswertungen durch Datenbanken und für die Einspeicherung und Verarbeitung in elektronische Systeme. Alle Rechte, auch die des auszugsweisen Nachdrucks, der fotomechanischen Wiedergabe (einschließlich Mikrokopie) sowie der Auswertung durch Datenbanken oder ähnliche Einrichtungen, vorbehalten.

Impressum:

Copyright © 2017 GRIN Verlag
Druck und Bindung: Books on Demand GmbH, Norderstedt Germany
ISBN: 9783668641389

Dieses Buch bei GRIN:

https://www.grin.com/document/413257

Susan Bailey

Does a distinctive Police culture exist in contemporary Policing

GRIN Verlag

GRIN - Your knowledge has value

Der GRIN Verlag publiziert seit 1998 wissenschaftliche Arbeiten von Studenten, Hochschullehrern und anderen Akademikern als eBook und gedrucktes Buch. Die Verlagswebsite www.grin.com ist die ideale Plattform zur Veröffentlichung von Hausarbeiten, Abschlussarbeiten, wissenschaftlichen Aufsätzen, Dissertationen und Fachbüchern.

Besuchen Sie uns im Internet:

http://www.grin.com/

http://www.facebook.com/grincom

http://www.twitter.com/grin_com

PART ONE:

Student and assessment details (*to be completed by student*)

PROGRAMME TITLE:	Criminological Studies with Social Sciences
MODULE TITLE:	Policing
ASSESSMENT TYPE (e.g. report, essay, etc)	Essay

The term 'police culture' is used to describe a complex set of beliefs and values held within the police force (Campeau, 2015). Culture has also been described as a patterned set of understandings to enable officers to cope, and adjust, to the pressures and tensions of front line policing (Maguire et al, 2002). There has been an increasing public interest in police culture over the past forty years, this interest is mainly due to public concerns, and therefore a discussion will be attempted, to look at if, and how police culture has changed. Events such as the Scarman Report (1981) have identified many of the problems within police culture, as has the Macpherson Report (1999), this essay will seek to evaluate whether these issues have been resolved in contemporary policing. A great number of scholars have studied police culture, such as, Reiner, Skolnick, Westley and Wilson, although most observational studies have focussed on uniformed officers, ignoring the behavioural differences and attitudes between "street cops" and "managerial cops" (Maguire et al, 2002).

Reiner (1985) famously summarised that police officers have core characteristics, he described the police as pessimistic, conservative, mission orientated, isolated, suspicious and masculine (Campeau, 2015). Policing has traditionally been a heterosexual, white male dominated occupation. With officers usually coming from an upper working class background, with very little formal education (Loftus, 2004). This created issues for individuals who did not fit these requirements due to sexuality, ethnicity or gender (Loftus, 2004). Stereotypical 'cop culture' has been described as almost a pure form of hegemonic masculinity (Newburn and Stanko, 1995). Officers are described to be aggressive, competitive and have a very patriarchal view towards women, often using racist or sexist language (Newburn and Stanko, 1995). Women encountered significant difficulty gaining acceptance into the police force as 'real' officers (Loftus, 2004). Members of the force become extremely loyal towards each other, and became isolated from others outside of the force. Westley (1970) suggested that police officers react this way for self-protection from the hostile world, as they see it. Joining together in isolation, and secrecy, from those outside of the police force.

Police culture has become a topic of interest since 1960, Westley (1970) being one of the earliest researchers into the subject (O'Neill et al, 2007). Westley (1970) noted that police officers appear to be have a very hostile view of the world around them, mainly because officers only come into contact with those that need to be policed, rather than those who need to be protected. The realities of police work, monotonous, mundane and unexciting, compared with the expectations of an action packed crime fighting day can also cause officers to develop a cynical view of the world around them (Banks, 2004).This cynical view could have a negative impact on the way police perform their duties, and view their job role (Banks, 2004).

The behaviour of the police force has led the public to believe that they are both racist and prejudiced towards minorities. Scarman (1981), was appointed to chair an investigation into the police force, following the Brixton Riots that took place between the 10th and 12th of April 1981 (Stout, 2010). The Scarman report (1981) described these incidents as the worst civil disorder outbreak in the 20th Century (Watson 2013). They occurred not only in Brixton but also in Manchester, Liverpool, West Midlands and Southall. These incidents, it was claimed by the public, were the result of the deteriorating relationship between the black community and the police, alongside high unemployment and existing social divisions (Bowling, 1998). Reports have since shown that the public, at the time, saw the police as racist and oppressive, the general consensus being that the police were contributing factors to the levels of violence that took place (Watson, 2013). The Moss Side Riots in 1981 were very similar, blaming police racism for the violence. The Moss Side community had consisted mainly of Asian and Caribbean communities, there had been reports of police abusing black youths before the attack began (Watson 2013).

The Scarman Report (1981) concluded that recognition and action was required to meet the needs, and special problems, of ethnic minorities (Bowling, 1998). Scarman (1981) reported that training was inadequate within the police and that racism, prejudice or discriminatory behaviour should become a disciplinary offence. A new monitoring and recording process for all police stop and search procedures, to eliminate accusations that ethnic minorities are searched more frequently (Stout, 2010). Scarman (1981) also recommended that the priority of the police force should be the maintenance of public safety, rather than just enforcing the law (Stout, 2010).

Although Scarman (1981) acknowledged that there was indirect discrimination within the police, his report did not go as far to say that the force was institutionally racist, however there was no policy in place to discourage racism (Stout, 2010).

The riots were a huge turning point for the police force, and the concept of public policing. As a result of the report there was to be an increased emphasis on community based policing in the years that followed (Watson, 2013). The Scarman Report (1981) was intended to produce a radical change within the police force, both with regards to race and equality (McLaughlin, 2006). However, a decade later it became apparent that racism was still prevalent within the force (McLaughlin, 2006).

Stephen Lawrence was a black teenager who was murdered in a racially motivated attack by a group of five white youths (Coates and Lawler, 2000). Nobody has ever been charged for his murder, and the investigation faced severe criticism. The Metropolitan Police force were subject to a public enquiry (Coates and Lawler, 2000). Macpherson (1999) conducted an inquiry into the investigation and produced a report. The report stated that the police attending the scene made little or no effort to pursue Lawrence's attackers (Giddens and Griffiths, 2006). The murder was not treat as urgent by the police, and as a result vital evidence was lost. Police surveillance of the incident was poorly organised. Witness statements were not taken seriously, and improper searches of the suspects houses were performed (Newburn, 2007). The Metropolitan police presumed that Lawrence was either a gang member, or had been involved in a street brawl, despite being an innocent victim of a racially motivated attack (Giddens and Griffiths, 2006). There was no evidence to suggest that senior officers attempted to intervene at any point, to rectify the mistakes that were made during the investigation (Newburn, 2007). Macpherson (1999) stated within his report that there had been fundamental errors without any doubt. The investigation was flawed by a combination of failure of leadership from senior officers, professional incompetence and institutional racism (Newburn, 2007).

The case of Stephen Lawrence opened a wider political debate into the methods of policing racial crime (Coates and Lawler, 2000). During the course of the investigation several police constables admitted the existence of racial attitudes amongst their officers, describing the problem as institutional racism (Coates and Lawler, 2000). The Macpherson Report (1999) identified institutional racism within the police force, and made seventy recommendations for improvement, including racial awareness training for all officers. Stronger disciplinary action was introduced for racist or discriminatory behaviour to remove racist officers. Furthermore, the report also expressed the need for a clearer definition of what constitutes a racist incident (Giddens and Griffiths, 2006). The police force had to show a commitment to employ more black and Asian officers. It was recommended that the home office should determine a nationally agreed procedure for dealing with complaints against the police (Joyce, 2001). The responsibility for dealing with a formal complaints procedure was to be with staff who were completely separate from the police force, to eradicate racism and bias from the police force (Joyce, 2012). The current system of police accountability, based on the Police Act (1964) provides a tripartite system of accountability (Kadar, 2001). The tripartite consists of three separate bodies, The Home Office, The Chief Constable and the local police authorities (Kadar, 2001). The responsibilities of the police force are distributed between the three to provide accountability to parliament through the home secretary (Joyce, 2012).

Documentaries that broadcast behaviour, usually hidden from the public have become a fascination in contemporary media (Chakraborti and Garland, 2009). In 2003 a documentary showed on BBC1 exposed extreme violent and racist attitudes by a number of police officers (Rowe, 2007).The documentary was filmed by an undercover reporter at a police training centre in Warrington. 'The Secret Policemen' shocked the public, as it showed trainee officers expressing support for far right political organisations and stereotyping (Chakraborti and Garland, 2009). More recently the Dispatches film 'Undercover Copper' released in 2006 revealed sexism, and pornography as continued features amongst officers within the police force (Rowe, 2007). The film also raised concerns of officers attitudes towards victims of rape, showing some male officers as behaving in an un-concerning manner towards victims (Rowe, 2007), it showed several examples of gender bias and prejudicial attitudes (Chakraborti and Garland, 2009). These documentaries gave an image to the public, that despite recommendations and apparent reform of the police force, nothing had changed. The police still displayed racist and inappropriate behaviour (Chan, 1996).

Recent documentaries and videos shared on social media have had a damaging impact on public perceptions of the police (Chakraborti and Garland, 2009). The term 'police culture' has been seen as a barrier for police reform, with many officers experiencing difficulty trying to get rid of their image of institutional prejudice. The new environment in which police officers now have to work in, police are less able to rely on 'canteen culture' to maintain solidarity (Campeau, 2015). The majority of the public have access to mobile phones with instant video recording, officers have reported that they are less likely to take part in activity that may be deemed as exciting or dangerous for fear of being filmed whilst violating a policy (Campeau, 2015).

It has been argued that an overarching analytical approach to police culture, has led to a 'cognitive burn in', the core features of distinctive police culture now serves as a collective imprint on how the police are now perceived (Campeau, 2015). Police culture is not necessarily a negative thing all of the time (Chan, 1996). Foster (2003) suggested that the term 'occupational culture' only focusses on the negative features of the officers personality. Whereas Waddington (1999) suggested that the police occupational culture may be a psychological form of defence, to help the officers, who deal with the problems and danger associated with the job on a daily basis. Police culture can be seen as being functional for officers who expose themselves to occupational hazards on a daily basis (Chan, 1996).

However, Skolnick (1996) was the first to propose the idea of a 'working personality', to explain police culture, his theory was generated by a combination of three elements of police work, danger, authority and efficiency (O'Neill et al, 2007). Skolnick (1996) suggested that police culture is a reflective of distinct cognitive tendencies in the police, as an occupational group. Skolnick (1996) and Westley work, although influential at the time has received much criticism. Their theory's oversimplified police relations with the public, and made no allowances for non-hostile encounters with the public (O'Neill et al, 2007). Reiner (2000) argues that although Skolnick (1996) did acknowledge that not all officers are alike in personality, he did not take account that his thesis could vary between forces and different departments of the police. Unlike

Westley's view that police culture is monolithic, Reiner (2010) stated that police culture is not monolithic. Similar core characteristics have been found in all police forces over four decades, work by Wilson (1968) showed different styles of policing within different police departments. Research suggests that cultural differences have been found within the same police force, according to rank and role (Maguire et al, 2002). Chief Inspector officers were found to have a different attitude to uniformed officers, and differences were also found with regards to the gender of officers. Leading to a common belief that there is a distinctive cultural difference between street cops and management cops (Maguire et al, 2002). The theory that police culture is monolithic, singular and unchanging is a misleading assumption, as there are cultural differences between forces (Chakraborti and Garland, 2009).The type of culture varies between forces, due to the different problems they face, the environment they work in and the legacies of their police history (Maguire, Morgan and Reiner, 2002).

Police organisations have undergone radical changes in the past twenty five years. Ten years after the Macpherson report, 67 of the 70 recommendations made, had been met either fully or partially. There has been diversity in recruitment, with higher numbers of female and ethnic minority officers now being employed (Campeau, 2015).Community based initiatives, and stringent training standards have been introduced. Most importantly there is a higher level of police accountability (Campeau, 2015). Although there were still some areas for concern within the police force (House of Commons: Home affairs committee 2009) black or ethnic people were still high in number in the stop and search statistics. Black and ethnic officers were still struggling to achieve promotion, and were more likely to be subject to disciplinary procedures (House of Commons: Home affairs committee 2009).

Researchers have argued that police culture does exist and that it is a necessary part of policing. It is a form of protection for officers facing occupational hazards on a daily basis. However, incidents have occurred within the police force that have displayed this culture as mainly negative and harmful to the reputation of the police force. The follow up to the Macpherson Report (2009) showed that the police force had not met their targets nationally for employing ethnic minority groups. Moreover, the report also showed that the stop and search records for black people were disproportionately high. Evidence has suggested that although police are more adequately trained, higher levels of women officers, and higher levels of police accountability, the home office still have concerns regarding the police force. Evidence has shown that the police have not transformed into the anti- racist, indiscriminate service required for today's multi-cultural society. The Scarman Report (1981) unveiled police racism as did the Macpherson report (1999). Similar recommendations were made by Macpherson for the police force 18 years after the Scarman Report (1981). The Brixton riots, and the Stephen Lawrence murder, were two very different events that share the same common features, police negligence and police racism. Although officers are no longer overtly racist, a widespread understanding of diversity has not been embedded within the police force. The contemporary documentaries shown in 2006 display the same level of police racial behaviour as was seen in 1981, suggesting that there is still a distinctive police culture within contemporary policing.

References

Banks, C. (2004) *Criminal justice ethics: Theory and practice*. Thousand Oaks, CA: Sage Publications (CA).

Bowling, B. (1998) Violent racism: Victimisation, policing and social context. New York: Clarendon Press.

Campeau, H. (2015)"*Police culture" at work: Making sense of police oversight*, British journal of criminology, 55(4), pp.669-687.doi:10. 1093/bjc/azu093.

Chakraborti, N. and Garland, J. (2009) *Hate crime causes and responses*. London: Sage Publications.

Coates, D. and Lawler, P.A. (Eds) (2000) *New labour into power*. Manchester University Press.

Giddens, A. and Griffiths, S. (2006) *Sociology* 5th edn. Cambridge: Polity Press.

House of Commons Home Affairs Committee (2009) *The Macpherson report- Ten years on: Twelfth report of session 2008-2009- report. Together with formal minutes, oral and written evidence* .United Kingdom: The Stationary office/Tso.

Joyce, P. (2012) *Criminal Justice*: An introduction 2nd edn. New York: Taylor & Francis.

Kadar, A. (2001 *Police in transition: Essays on the police forces in transition countries*. Edited by Andras Kadar. Budapest: Central European University press.

Loftus, B. (2012) *Police culture in a changing world*. Oxford University Press.

Maguire, M., Morgan, R. and Reiner, R. (Eds) (2002) The Oxford handbook of criminology. 3rd edn. Oxford, England: Oxford university press.

McLaughlin, E. (2006) *The new policing*. London: Sage Publications Ltd. United Kingdom.

Morgan, R. and Newburn, T. (1997) *The future of policing*. Oxford, (England): Oxford University Press.

Myhill, A. and Bradford, B. (2013) *Overcoming cop culture. Organisational Justice and police officers attitudes towards the public*, Policing: An International journal of police strategies & management, 36(2), pp338-356. Doi: 10. 1108/113639511311329732.

Newburn, T. and Stanko, E.A. (Eds) (1995) *Just boys doing business?. Men, masculinities and crime.* London: Routledge.

O'Neill, M., Marks, M. and Singh, A-M. (2007) *Police occupational culture: New debates and directions.* Amsterdam: Elsevier Jai.

Rowe, M. (Eds) (2007) *Policing beyond Macpherson: Issues in policing, race and society.* Portland, OR: Willan Publishing.

Stout, B. (2010) *Equality and diversity in policing.* Exeter: Learning matters.

Watson, A. (2013) *Gravity and mind: Human response to tectonic stress.* United Kingdom: AL writing.

BEI GRIN MACHT SICH IHR WISSEN BEZAHLT

- Wir veröffentlichen Ihre Hausarbeit, Bachelor- und Masterarbeit

- Ihr eigenes eBook und Buch - weltweit in allen wichtigen Shops

- Verdienen Sie an jedem Verkauf

Jetzt bei www.GRIN.com hochladen und kostenlos publizieren